WHAT DO WE STILL WANT TO DO?

Exploding
assumptions
about
women's
lives
after 60

IDA • 2

FOREWORD

Welcome to the second book from The Ida Project – a network that brings together women over 60 to make connections and share stories of their lives. The project was the idea of three friends – Belinda Budge, Ann Treneman and Vicky Wilson – all in their late 60s. It came about when we realised that we had been talking a lot about the new discoveries and challenges we were facing, and wondered if we could involve other women in a creative conversation about this stage of our lives.

The three of us met back in 1986 on a Women's Studies MA course at the University of Kent and subsequently set up a feminist publishing company, Scarlet Press, with the aim of provoking debate and exploring issues we felt had been underrepresented in the mainstream. We took the name 'Ida' from New York feminist and activist artist Ida Applebroog (1929–2023), who in the late 1970s circulated her work by sending self-published pamphlets to friends through the post. Our initial call-out for people to join The Ida Project therefore came in the form of a postcard, in homage to the idea that not everything needs to be online.

The title of our first book, *Is This What We Expected?*, was drawn from the issues raised by the women who responded to the postcards, which invited them to join a 'creative conversation about women's lives from their 60s to their 90s'. While the postcards were sent only to friends (or friends of friends), the popularity of *Is This What We Expected?* means our network has expanded rapidly.

The present, longer volume, with its question, *What Do We Still Want To Do?*, follows on from some of the issues raised. Here you'll find tales of forging new lives and of reconciliation with the past. There are accounts of renewed political engagement and artistic fulfilment. There are stories of looking deeper into what is around us as well as branching out to explore new territory, emotional, intellectual and physical.

We believe that every woman can be a writer, so every one of the 50 contributions we received has been published here. We asked for 300 words, but when people wrote longer and we felt unable to cut their stories, we opted to give them two pages. Uniquely, Lindsay MacRae has two pieces as we couldn't resist including the poem she wrote to perform at the first live Ida event at the Brighton Dome in June 2024.

We found the range of experiences, perspectives and attitudes in the accounts we were sent by turns moving, provocative and inspiring. We hope that collectively they will challenge expected narratives and sometimes pernicious assumptions about older women – hence our retention of the subtitle from volume 1, 'Exploding assumptions about women's lives after 60'.

We thank everyone who responded to our invitation to contribute. Please get in touch if you would like to join the conversation, and we will continue to keep you all informed about whatever happens next.

Belinda, Ann and Vicky
info@theidaproject.com

CONTENTS

Gus Watcham · Tidy	9
Lou Beckerman · Welcome To The Now	10
Carolan Evans · No More Norms	12
Helen Genty · What Do I Want?	13
Holly Aylett · Where To Go From Here?	14
Judy Ironside MBE · If Not Now, When?	16
Liz Hall · The List	17
Kerry Kilner · The Alchemy Of New Beginnings	18
Belinda Budge · Reframing The Question	19
Joan Byrne · Wanting More	20
Bibi Brown · And Why Not?	21
Gail Chester · What Do I Still Want To Do?	22
Nicky Packer · Say Yes To More!	24
Lindsay Macrae · Favourite Things	26
Pol Marson · This Perfect Week	27
Karen Wade · The Aquatic Calendar Girls?	28
Barbara Riley · Priorities?	30
Cindy Etherton · Please And Thank You	31
Usha Letchumanan-Pearce · Reclaiming My Name	32
Alanna McIntyre · What I Still Want To Do	34
Bridget Farrands · Living With Purpose	35
Fran Ellery · What I Really, Really Want	36
Margaret Cooter · Stop Moaning And Do Something	38
Kim Hope · Becoming A 'Craftivist'	39
Liz Puttick · Embracing Activism	40
Gerrie ter Haar · Real Life	42
Ruth Hilton · I Just Want To Carry On	43
Margie Mitchell · Old Bag, New Bag	44

Vicky Wilson · Zero Waste	46
Ariana Gee · Girls R Us	47
Helen Aguirre · The Ofrenda	48
Sue Blundell · The Mixture As Before	50
Katherine Ukleja · A Legacy Of Awe And Sorrow	51
Em Sawday · A Line Of Strong Women	52
Marcelle Delvaux-Abbott · Fun When You Turn 60	54
Sally Spinks · Changes	56
Lindsay Macrae · Now We Are 63	57
Grishma Sutaria · Retirement	58
Marie Mulvey-Roberts · Is There Life After Retirement?	59
Helen Lindsay-Breakspear · Time and Words: Emerita	60
Fiona Duby · Who Knows?	61
Eileen Campbell · Living Creatively	62
Vicci Johnson · Happy Being Me	64
Mary Allen · Simplicity, Patience, Compassion	65
Debbie Thorpe · A More Centred Life	66
Midori Nishikawa · Bionic Woman	67
Wanda Whiteley · The Gate In The Wall	68
Nancy Charley · What A Gift!	70
Joy Fisher · Reverse Bucket List	71
Ann Treneman · Out!	74

GUS WATCHAM TIDY

What I want to do now is to keep my desk tidy. Or to be able to see the desk surface, or most of it. My workroom is very small and I'm an untidy person, so for years I've been opening the door, throwing stuff towards the desk and letting it lie. When there was just a lot of stuff on the desk it was OK, but then the desk disappeared and thus it stayed.

A friend told me once that your subconscious always knows where everything is; that it does feverish inventories even when you're asleep. I find this horrifying, but I'm afraid it might be true.

Not long ago I jumped out of bed knowing I had to fix it and started tidying there and then. It turned out to be a process more than an event, but gradually the desk surface reappeared, and with it various items that either I'd thought were lost forever, or had forgotten existed – some of which I liked better that way. I rediscovered filing.

A lot of bags have gone to recycling and the bin. I don't feel tidier now, but my emotions seem to run freer – I'm angrier, sadder, more immediately open to joy, as if I've tapped a seam. I think I'm a bit braver. I have no explanation for this. The desk stays vaguely clear most of the time. Not better, not worse, just different.

LOU BECKERMAN
WELCOME TO THE NOW

Welcome to the Now. Allow
no hesitation
for more rumination,
a safer situation or
inspiring quotation.
This is your station. This is your stop.
Just mind the gap as you climb off.

You can delay, postpone, press pause, atone,
make 'To Wait' your occupation,
'To Defer' a vocation,
as though Procrastination
is a final destination,
but this is your stop. Step off.
Welcome to the Now.

Your turbulent train of thought
brought you here – fraught,
caught in its whirling wheels of
worry and hurry,
frenzy and flurry –
side-tracked, derailed,
dreams failed.

All things come to those who wait...
Right?
(*So when did you last see swine in flight?*)
You can wait for tomorrow or for Godot,
perhaps a blue moon, life to attune, or be immune,
hang on, hold fast,
grow a crust, perhaps rust.

The time is never entirely proper
to drop off, or stop or
take off
at a tangent
but this is your
perfect moment.
This is your stop so step off.
Welcome to the Now.

Detach from your luggage
the deadweight tonnage of
disturbing drama, chaotic karma
and imagined umbrage.
This is your
If-Not-Now-Then-When-Or-How
stop.
Step off, meet and greet
your side-lined sweet
Self.
Welcome to the Now.

CAROLAN EVANS NO MORE NORMS

Life is a journey, mapped and measured in time, seasons, thresholds, expectations…

When I was small, I was often asked, 'What do you want to be when you grow up?' That was easy: a ballet dancer, or failing that a trapeze artiste or a circus bareback rider. I was briefly a ballet dancer.

When I reached 60, I was asked, 'What will you do now that you are retired?' More difficult. What? Retired? No, I've still so much to do, students to teach, clients to see. In my 70s, a serious accident in the Andes forced the issue and I retired with rather bad grace.

Now in my 80s, I'm asked, 'What do you still want to do?' Am I grown up enough yet? That seems the hardest question and is an ongoing enquiry. At this point there are no more norms, no maps to follow, just an inevitable end point. The urge for travel, exploration and adventure is still there, though the impetus is weaker now, the bucket list shorter, and I am being nudged more towards small joys and contentment. But is this enough?

Age brings perspective and enables the patterns and thresholds of life to be seen: the disasters that were blessings in disguise, the sudden unearned good fortune, the intuitive decision that opened a whole new vista. It also brings questions. Who am I now when I have no job title, or a hat to wear that defines a role in life? What masks am I discarding and which do I still want to hide behind? Dare I risk being entirely, freely myself after a lifetime of doing what was expected?

HELEN GENTY WHAT DO I WANT?

Having witnessed my parents' descent into frailty and vulnerability, I am increasingly aware that life is a treasure – this 'wild and precious life', as Mary Oliver calls it. The decade from 60 to 70 is likely to be the best of what is to come. But how should I use it?

A friend said she was going to do fewer things and go more deeply into them. But I feel too greedy to let things go. I still want to play at dressmaking, gardening and singing, do yoga and take up the recorder. Plus, I find myself hungrily consuming a diet of spiritual and theological writing, most recently Eckhart and Creation Theology. Then not having made great provision for old age, it is likely I will still be working through this decade. The alternative would be a frugality I'm not ready to embrace. There is a view that we have many 'I's that all want different things. But mine are all competing.

In my work as a therapist, I use the '90 looking back' exercise: imagine yourself at 90 and ask what you would need to have done to feel your life was complete. Probably not spend more time at your computer! For Jung, the path of life was to become the person you were meant to be, and I'm still exploring that. Maybe I was meant to be a bumbler with a range of interests rather than devoting myself to a single skill or path, like writing or painting?

The idea that people won't remember what you did, but how you made them feel, would encourage us to work not on our achievements, but on our way of being. My mother, at the age of 95, is loved for her humanity and peacefulness. Well done her.

HOLLY AYLETT
WHERE TO GO FROM HERE?

What do I still want to do? There's a clock ticking in this question, though time is not linear, rather a definition of how we choose to live our lives. I've been caught short once, and severely, by illness and the prospect then of only two more years – absurdity. Its shadow brought uncertainty and the urgency to prioritise: not so much to focus on what I can do – in our 60s the fabric is richly woven – but what I can do best. And what will I regret not having done when the time comes?

I started in theatre and long to use my body again to express the emotion of my older selves, perhaps with an Indian theatre group for a month in the forests around Chennai. If so, the chance to pick up the trail of Archana, one of the wonderful women I've filmed, who stitched women's lives into embroidered panels and took their stories from a tiny village in Bihar to the Museum Mile of New York. Another drift is to head solo to Iran, to catch the scents of its ancient wisdoms despite the noise of today's menace.

When you're young, you're trying to work out what to do with your life. In your 60s, there's a sense of consolidation. There also seems to be something of a 40-year loop, spinning events, songwriters and social movements I've known back into my present, albeit through new filters: the unravelling legacies of the fall of the Berlin Wall, the wilderness of Joni Mitchell's lyrics, racisms revisited. There's knowledge to be affirmed in our historical tales/tails and a clout which experience brings to oppose myopic politics, injustice and the violation of genocide.

History will be repeating itself long after I'm gone, assuming humanity hangs on to its place on this rock, spinning out in our billion-starred galaxy. Years ago, the nineteen-year-old son of a Mexican friend came to stay on his way to an artist's studio in Madrid. 'What would you like to do to make the most of your time in London?' I asked. 'I'm trying to drop out of time,' he replied dryly.

Such rhythms are hard to listen to in the din of imperatives to earn, to care for, to project-manage – the drill of a woman's life in action. So now I wish to brave silence in writing, in music, in the more resonant space of a room of my own.

JUDY IRONSIDE MBE
IF NOT NOW, WHEN?

Approaching 80, my thoughts often turn to energy: how much do I have and when do I acknowledge that this commodity will not always be abundant?

I have lived my life always considering what I would regret if I did not attempt it rather than holding back through fear or risk of failure. I have had at least two long and successful careers and brought up five children, while always working in the arts or creative industries. I have skied down mountains, trekked in Bhutan, spent time in deserts, nearly frozen, and swum in many oceans (despite my terror of jellyfish!). I remain curious to travel but not with the same fearless enthusiasm, compounded by my great concern for the environment.

I have always focused on sharing our stories and this has taken me from an early career as a drama therapist to founding and then working on the UK Jewish Film Festival for almost 30 years. This year, however, I plan to embark on training to become a Celebrant. I am excited about the idea of creating ceremonies and bringing my lived experiences to this new career.

I avoid the shadow curled in the corner... maybe it is waiting to pounce...? 'Hello dark shadow' – I need at least to acknowledge that ill-health and death could have power over my life. For now, however, I choose to love and live my life to the full. In time we will meet, but until then I will keep living and planning.

LIZ HALL THE LIST

I went to the store and I ordered a blood-red sunrise.
I went to the store and I ordered a blood-red sunrise
 and a painless death.
I went to the store and I ordered a blood-red
 sunrise, a painless death and an off-shore
 wind with a peeling wave.

I went to the store and I ordered a pair of
 non-clicking knees, some good cholesterol and
 1.2 kilograms of normal cognitive function.

I went to the store and I ordered:
An exceptional sex life
A trip to Nepal
Nine thousand downward-facing dogs
A sell-out solo show at the Edinburgh Fringe
Green tea and warm touch in the morning calm
 of white sheets
A sudden and unexplained mastery of the piano
Watching cranes dance at Gallocanta in the late sun
Better health for my daughter
Twenty music festivals (*with ear protectors*)
And world peace.

I went to the store and I ordered a visibility cloak,
 a spotlight, a loud speaker and a buzzcut.
I went to the store and I ordered friends, wine
 and good food.
I went to the store and I ordered potential fulfilled.

I went to the store and told them – I'll collect it
 tomorrow.
I went to the store and told them – put it on my tab.

KERRY KILNER
THE ALCHEMY OF NEW BEGINNINGS

The glaze and clay of the funerary urn vitrifies to ceramic and glass in the dark space of the kiln. An alchemical fusion of intent and chance. The studio, blue and bold in the garden, welcomes me daily as I embrace the alchemy of a practice now central to this third phase of what may be a lifespan of some 90 years (if I follow my parents).

This life I see now as a triangle. The first 30, slanting from apex to the left corner: surviving childhood, adolescence, the catastrophe of following others' expectations, of early mothering and not mothering, fear; the second 30, that foundation line, spent career-wise, parenting, enduring the academy and plagued by imposter syndrome, illness, and, finally, at 59, an escape from the bounds of that life and from a country in which I felt deep disappointment.

As chance would have it, Covid-19 locked me down in rural southwest Ireland, where an old farmhouse welcomed and encouraged me to transform, not only it, but myself. Now I reach towards the zenith of the triangle through a life of experimental creativity. Here, at 62, I am a potter, ceramicist, a 'kiln-er', following a youthful dream and making a future marked by delight, perpetual learning, and the wisdom of mud. The funerary urn with its star-rise lid, made by instinct at a time of endings – my old life, my mother's life, and a failing relationship – is symbolic of my transformation to this: my own creative life, with none but my own, and the clay's, expectations to meet.

BELINDA BUDGE
REFRAMING THE QUESTION

I don't know why, but for as long as I can remember, I have always asked myself: 'If I died tomorrow, will I have done everything I wanted to do?' Now, as I write, I think it is an odd question for a child to ask, but the very oddness prompts memories of the death of my younger brother, Simon, who died when he was just a few months old. I was three, and for many years I took on my mother's pain at her son's death.

I didn't recognise how the question became mine. Ever at the forefront of my mind, it has meant that I have always striven to keep moving and to be in the world. In some ways it has been a heavy burden; in others it has kept me conscious and driven me towards embracing new experiences, pushing myself when I felt like hiding away, engaging with what was around me and always expanding the space I was in. I guess it has given me a wonderful zest for life.

Now in my late 60s, answering the question 'What do I still want to do?' has unexpectedly reframed the question in my heart and this is liberating. I am still moving forward, but I am not striving. I finally have a joyful answer to the question:

The object isn't to make art, it's to be in that wonderful state which makes art inevitable.
Robert Henri, painter

JOAN BYRNE WANTING MORE

My business crashed just before I reached the age of 60. En route to Job Centre appointments, I would take photographs. It helped that my local patch is in a wondrous part of London. I became a street photographer, exhibited and even won an award. Along with this, I began to mix with artists, and my social life was enriched by Private Views and fascinating conversations.

Simultaneously, I began to take poetry seriously. I was lucky enough to join with two other poets, and together we became the Rye Poets. We have performed for many audiences, and we are still at it, as it were.

I can't quite account for when my focus moved from photography to making collages. It may have had something to do with becoming older; in my mid-70s, I can't run as fast! This summer I was fortunate to have a solo exhibition, and following that an invitation to show work at a prestigious arts venue after the curator spotted my collages on Instagram.

I'm not a natural at art. A school report shows my mark as 35%... I know... don't praise the child. For most of my life, pressure to make art led only to embarrassment. Without these extra years, I reckon my elbows would have remained pinned to my sides.

As to the future, I want more. I want to make more edgy collages, write more poems, perform more and make an impact. By that, I mean no one lives in a vacuum. I want to engage with the state of things: commenting, shaking things up. And, boy, do they need a shake.

BIBI BROWN AND WHY NOT?

A big want-to-do for me was to gather up all the children in the world who were trapped in violence and poverty. Gather them up, and put them on my grandma-lap. So I did – through a book, almost ready now and with the title *The World According To Bokkie* (or TWA2B as it has become known).

Bokkie became my alter ego. She could travel time and space, through heart–mind projection, and go wherever she was pulled. She would concentrate her heart and send a blast of love to children usually inaccessible to outside help. They would receive this gift and take strength from it. Bokkie also taught young people who clamoured to help little ones: they became her heart warriors, roaming the world in the same way. Bokkie called her service www.looming. A world-wide web, weaving love into dark places.

As I was writing, I would read extracts to my trusted critics. Each said: you must record this. And so I did, through a visit to a dear friend in Spain who is a master of recording. An artist friend will draw the cover illustration for both versions but I'm not looking for a publisher. This is a DIY job. Why not?

I love the characters. They have come alive. In my imagination, the book has become a film – made in Japan by artistic wizards. It has become a stage play – magical and orchestrated. I can see the scenes unfolding: the little lost ones in the centre, huddled together – and then breathing as they are reached.

Why not? What do we really know about how things happen? And of course we old ones can dream big dreams too.

GAIL CHESTER
WHAT DO I STILL WANT TO DO?

This
This!
This is what I want to do
More of this
More writing
More thinking
More time to focus on my own thoughts
My own needs
More time to reflect on how well I have already done
Less time being assailed by self-doubt
Less time fighting so other people can get their needs met
No more time responding to other people's urgent pleas for help
Even when I know that ignoring them is not realistic

I want to stop feeling guilty and selfish for writing the above sentences
I want to scream 'Fuck you all, I'm off'
And mean it

Mean the 'I'm off' bit
Not so much the 'Fuck you all' bit
Because I do still care immensely about all the people whose needs have eaten away at my life and my resolve to be a fulfilled writer
But I want others to care too
And I don't just mean the others who are already doing their best in difficult circumstances

I mean the perpetrators of neoliberalism, the
     advocates of austerity
Those are the people I will no longer allow to hold
     me back
The apparently faceless ones
The ones we cannot name

But they have names, they have faces
They don't live round the corner
But they are still people
They have the capacity to make different decisions

The question is:
How to make them do it?

I want to believe that my writing will contribute
But you know what?
Even if it makes no difference at all to anybody else
I still intend to write
For me

NICKY PACKER SAY YES TO MORE!

My 50s dawned with plans for a new career and expanding horizons, fuelled by optimism at my children's growing independence as they bumbled through their teenage years. What happened instead was seemingly endless loss and insecurity, living in what effectively became a war zone, both at work and at home.

To my amazement, my friends and my own dogged placing of one foot in front of another have carried me to what now feels like a joyous second teenagerhood – even if I no longer have the years ahead I once took for granted. To feel so free and full of an appetite for life is intoxicating, sweetened by contrast with what had led me to this opening of new doors.

A few years ago I recognised that it was up to me to colour in the shape of my life. I grasped the mantra 'say yes to more', writing it down one New Year and putting it in my knicker drawer, so each day would start with this reminder. When I was asked to go body-boarding – something my kids had done while I sat and watched – the message in the knicker drawer called to me and 'OK, I'll give it a go' fell out of my mouth. I found I loved the thrill of the rush and the drug-like compulsion to try the next wave. I felt so alive!

Since then I have paraglided off a mountainside in Colombia after a lifetime of fearing heights, travelled to South America and India, where I was a wise owl for younger travellers in hostels, got back on my bike, and danced the night away in clubs where younger women revel in my freedom and confidence. I've continued to discover what my ageing body can do, testing myself in ballet and contemporary dance classes and making warm friendships along the way. I've held parties and discovered my own style of entertaining, lapped up live theatre, dance, music and comedy (it beats sitting at home in front of the TV), and joined a supper club of complete strangers to sample the diversity of cultures and cuisines in Bristol – a city I feel can be a home for this new phase of my life. And I do all this on a tight budget, buying almost everything through charity shops and growing what food I can.

I don't recognise this mover and shaker, but maybe in my past my courage and energy were all channelled towards others and now I am becoming more at ease with the idea of putting myself in the sunlight alongside them?

On the outside I may be ageing, but on the inside I'm just taking off again. I've tasted life and can happily say I want more of the same as well as the unknown unknowns, while my body and mind will allow it. How lucky am I?

LINDSAY MACRAE FAVOURITE THINGS
(Kind of to the tune of 'My Favourite Things' from *The Sound of Music*; written to perform at the first live Ida event at the Brighton Dome, June 2024)

Afternoon movies and talking to strangers
Shocking my kids with outrageous behaviour
Dancing while sober and not in a club
This is a list of the things I now love:

Being alive – sifting hard fact from fiction
Knowing most drama takes place in the kitchen
Having my own teeth, house keys and specs
Friends who aren't bitchy, much better sex

Children (now adults) who like me and speak
Longing no more for the end of each week
Ordering just starters (they're more than enough)
More space for people instead of more stuff
Getting past go when the going gets tough

Gardens and trees now seem more appealing
Than any activity which involves kneeling
Loving my body – it got me this far
Giving up high heels and sometimes a bra

Not giving a damn if I'm out on a limb
I care more about grammar than having to win
Waving not drowning (I've learnt how to swim)

When I was young I thought I was the story
(Give me an Oscar, bathe me in glory)
It's a relief to be older and know that I'm not
I'm content to be sane still – a part of the plot.

POL MARSON THIS PERFECT WEEK

Monday 8.00: Train from Redland, Bristol, to Euston, London, carrying four bags: dance gear, overnight bag, knitting bag (for my yet-to-be-born first grandchild), handbag. A week of contemporary dance classes – yeah!

11.30: Arrive at The Place, where 28 of us gather for the first Over-60s Dance session. I take a deep breath as I move into my place and the class begins. At this moment, there is nowhere on earth I would rather be.

13.00: Coffee in the oldest pedestrianised street in England, then off to the John Lewis sale and rooftop café with Jennifer.

17.00: Return to Pam's flat. Alcohol-free wine… I'm getting used to it.

Tuesday 9.00: Breakfast at Café Continenté: French toast, blueberries and crème fraîche, accompanied by a flat white. They remember my order from last time.

10.30: Full day of dance classes… already I don't mind having got off the tube at the wrong station. Afternoon session is Alston Repertoire to Steve Reich music: 'How small a thought it takes to fill a whole life'. Affecting.

Wednesday: Café Continenté – dance – lunch – dance. Such friendly, interesting, diverse people in the class. Good to be together.

Thursday 10.30: Photoshoot for dance-class website – 'be playful', great FUN. Two more classes.

Friday 10.30: Dance class.

12.00: Goodbyes and back to Bristol.

Because… It is intellectually and physically demanding, collective, creative. Always.

KAREN WADE
THE AQUATIC CALENDAR GIRLS?

We are beginning to learn that our brains are hardwired to react positively to water and that being near it can calm and connect us, increase innovation and insight, and even heal what's broken.
Wallace J. Nichols, *Blue Mind* (2014)

The result? Joy.

Well at least for me and for every rower I have spoken to – and in this final sprint of my life, I intend to spread the word.

I think the wish lists of women over 60 are not dissimilar to those of men: physical health, mental health, proximity to, and good things for, our family and friends.

But we also need purpose – and we need energy.

For me, the issue is not a woman's age (which cannot be altered), but the fact that we rarely see women of our age doing things, saying things, raising expectations. Role models are rare – and we can't all be Helen Mirren. We complain about being invisible, but we do so from beneath a cloak of preconceptions, stereotypes and tradition.

At our age we have so much wisdom and experience, so many talents to share, so many ways to *normalise* the idea of older women doing wonderful, inspiring and visible things.

My particular, peculiar talent seems to be encouraging others to experience the joy of rowing in late adulthood: to get women on the water, to 'have a go', not at an elite level, but in a keeping-fit, enjoying-the-camaraderie and staying-upbeat kind of way.

I began spreading the word by writing articles, and then founded Henley Rowing Association. Recently I learned that marine biologist and author Wallace J. Nichols (see above) claimed that 'neuroscience confirms that storytelling has unique power to change opinions and behaviour' – and that has set me off on a whole new tributary: writing based on eight diverse, aquatic Calendar Girls (one for each seat in a boat).

I hope to finish it soon. It's my tuppence-worth at trying to increase our visibility. Yes, in Lycra, on the water, because so much of what we learn there can be transferred to everyday life, to help us to become the best version of ourselves, at any age.

BARBARA RILEY PRIORITIES?

The answer has, somewhat magically, appeared all by itself. The priorities have prioritised themselves.

It is often said that a post-60s woman is voiceless, invisible, disempowered. I disagree. A woman in her 60s and beyond is surely the opposite of these things – it is time, and we hopefully have the time, to celebrate voice, vision and strength. The female self.

In Walt Whitman's 'Song of Myself' (from *Leaves of Grass*) the American poet speaks of detail – of looking down, of observing, of every atom, of beauty and the 'watching and wondering at it'. Once, a long time ago, I was a high jumper – literally, and, I suppose, figuratively. I was in the game, raising the bar, looking up – loving it. I was in the field with what Walt Whitman termed 'linguists and contenders'. My academic game was all about the words: the unravelling of texts and the re-ravelling of literary criticism – working it up.

But Whitman also called the field of linguists and contenders a 'fog' – implying a mistiness, an ethereality. The priority now, in my 60s, is clarity, being closer to home, closer to the ground. Literally and figuratively. Now I want to slow (but not slow down) to look at the leaves of grass, dissipate the fog – exciting as it was (and hoping I can return to it from time to time). I want to connect with the tangible earth and sing a song of detail – of every atom.

I contend with my seedlings now, working them up, talking to them – my neighbour says that's just fine. And I agree. The 'field' after 60 does not feel smaller; it feels richer and deeper. Fertile.

CINDY ETHERTON
PLEASE AND THANK YOU

John Donne reminded us that it is astonishing to be alive, and that life calls on us to remain astonished. So far, that sums up my feelings. Each year since I turned 40 has been better than the last; with a few exceptions, there's been an upward trend. I enjoy the space and freedom of being over 60, unencumbered by the norms conformed to in past decades.

If there's time, I want to blend the old and the new into interesting shapes and live to see what that looks like. I plan for as long as possible to appreciate and respect the people and places of my life. My mother's last words, spoken in February 2023, were 'thank you'. Please may they be my last words too.

I wish I could see my son again before I die, although it seems unlikely.

Maintaining the ability to prepare food for family, friends and other animals, served with a side of delightful conversation to express love, is a priority. All my life I lived under many false names until 2012, when I married and took my wife's name, which I'll sign with a proud smile until I can't anymore.

I'm trying to worry less about politics and society, and I won't be abseiling down the tallest building in my home city again. I still want to write, love, dream, romance, be thankful and stay open to changes in perspective.

Because I treasure independence of mind and good listening, I hope to encourage both in others. To many women, we are *the future*, and we need to shine a bright light ahead.

USHA LETCHUMANAN-PEARCE
RECLAIMING MY NAME

Standing on the threshold of three score and eight, reflecting on 'What do I still want to do?', takes me back to the past, a life of ebbs and flows, pain and pleasure. As the saying goes: for a thousand joys, a thousand sorrows. An immigrant, I have called England home for 40 years. Throughout this journey, numerous significant events have given shape to the person I am.

Perhaps the first significant experience was encountering subtle racism as a young university researcher and having to make the difficult decision to drop my maiden surname and use my married name instead. Letchumanan was clunky, and a give-away that I was a foreigner. Being a Pearce was easier to get past receptionists in a study involving general practitioners. Race was an issue, as ever. Equally shaping was having a profoundly deaf child and fighting for her cause every step of the way, determined that she would not be ghettoised, but have the widest possible choices.

Hence, I do not approach my 60s as a blank canvas but as a continuation of my history. With the same fluidity, expansiveness and curiosity, I would like to remain open to opportunities in whatever form they might present themselves and be immersed in a creative life in the fullest sense: aspiring for a way of being rather than doing, allowing for ambiguity and the spaces in between to exist.

Aiming not for grand gestures or being limited by what 'should be' but being appreciative of the small things in life. Regardless of age or the vicissitudes of life, to be in the moment and accept with humility what the future holds, in the knowledge that I have the love of a wonderful family and friends. To live by what Rumi wrote:

Let yourself be silently drawn by the strange pull of what you really love. It will not lead you astray. In the silence, there is a sacred mystery, a path that shows the way not with words but with the heart's yearning.

And perhaps even reclaim my name.

ALANNA MCINTYRE
WHAT I STILL WANT TO DO

Now in my late 70s, I want to continue to lead the life I've created, a routine that keeps me involved with my community and my family. It's a structure that suits my needs.

My garden is my haven, mainly self-seeded and cut and trimmed once a year. The rest of the time, I tidy and enjoy the surprises that pop up. In autumn I always plant bulbs, so spring brings a burst of colour.

With the help of my children, I want to continue to clear the unwanted stuff from my loft. Possessions are no longer particularly important to me – I prefer experiences. I live in Brighton and I enjoy the Brighton Fringe festival and the Rotunda Theatre, where I've made friends with the owners and been able to chat to some of the performers.

I fundraise for a Brighton-based charity called Indian Futures that empowers young women in the remote area of Tamil Nadu in Southern India by sponsoring them to pursue the further education of their choice. Some of the fundraising events feature readings of pieces produced in a writing group I facilitate in a sheltered home. I also run mindfulness sessions in the Brighton suburb of Whitehawk, highlighting the importance of self-care, of appreciating the present moment and of living in the now. Like Tamil Nadu, Whitehawk is an underprivileged area where I can work to help the community.

For the future, I hope I will be able to continue to help others and to be kind – as well as saying 'No' when I need to so I don't risk overdoing it!

BRIDGET FARRANDS
LIVING WITH PURPOSE

It seems every generation has lived its old age differently from the one before. My grandparents, born in the late 19th century, saw old age as a time to do very little. They sat a lot, listened to the radio and did crosswords. My parents, born around World War I, thought golf and gardening should fill retirement.

My own baby-boomer generation was supposed to do everything differently. So how is this phase of life going for us? Certainly the biggest change I notice in myself and my friends is our refusal to contemplate a life of not very much happening. It's as though living must still have some purpose, because without that we would be living the life of the already dead.

For me, now in my 70s, that purpose involves the need to go on being relevant by contributing my experience and skills to causes and people who find them useful. This is not so different from my working life as a consultant and coach, which has been so satisfying I am reluctant to give it up. But now I need to find other ways to put my experience and skills to good use – not least because of a widespread prejudice that people over 60 are incapable of contributing value. Things I still want to do include writing another book, becoming an artist and being able to celebrate 60 years of marriage, all of which would make me feel my life has purpose, relevance and stimulus.

I've also become interested in exploring how others navigate this phase of life, so I'm researching via interviews to see if there are patterns I can identify. So far the findings are intriguing!

FRAN ELLERY
WHAT I REALLY, REALLY WANT

What do I want, do I really, really want? I don't know! Lots and lots? Nothing? A little bit more of the same? Less?

I think...

I want to be FREE! But I don't want to be cut loose. I want to rid myself of guilt and a sense of obligation (but I want to hold on to the love, closeness and warmth I feel with my partner, my family and my long-term friends).

I want to be mobile and free from pain. But I accept that I can't do many of the things I could when I was younger. I am, and look, old now. (Please don't ever let me wear lilac and beige and look like I've just stepped off a coach, though.)

I want to have fun! To go out and dance and sing and swim and walk and paint and play music and hang out at home and with friends, old and new.

I want to have time to read, shut out the world, lie down on the sofa and immerse myself in a great novel like I used to. (But I also love the fact that I don't have to finish a badly written book I'm not interested in or enjoying.)

I want not to work so much but not to give up. (Because I can, because it's interesting, because it keeps me connected to the world and younger generations, because I'm flattered that I'm still asked to, because it supplements my pension, because, because...)

I'm not really bothered about travelling and seeing new places (except New York and Cuba, though maybe too late now). I certainly DO NOT want to go on a cruise. I want time to go inwards and revisit places and experiences from my rich, adventurous and, at times, scary past. What memories – many shared with people still in my life now, some (an increasing number) with those I've lost.

I want to find some sort of peace and contentment (but not be complacent). I still want to rage and take action against violence and discrimination against women, communities and whole countries. In the 1980s I received death threats for supporting Palestine, was thrown out of the House of Commons for demonstrating against anti-abortion laws and was attacked by National Front members for distributing Anti-Nazi League leaflets in Brick Lane.

I wish I could say those battles have been won. For some, and in many ways, of course things have improved. But I know that for many they've got worse. Despite all the so-called progress and connectedness (some of which is real, heartwarming and cause for optimism), life in the 21st century really has no common meaning. Just as in previous times, it depends entirely on who and where we are.

I want not to despair at the state of the world and what's in store for future generations. I want to have faith that there will be radical change, that young people will reject rampant capitalism and the post-World War II obsession with property and status. I want those of us in the West to be prepared not to have what our and previous entitled generations have come to expect.

What do I want? What do I really, really want?

I really want things to get better...

MARGARET COOTER
STOP MOANING AND DO SOMETHING

It is the 11th hour: for me and many others in their mid-70s, as health gets more precarious year by year; for the planet, in all things climatic and ecological; and for humanity, which seems to be entering a dark, divisive era.

We are acting as if the future will be much like the past and we are changing very little in how we go about our daily lives. Many people have said, 'Hope for the best, but prepare for the worst'. The worst, of course, will fall on younger generations.

It's a big challenge, as we grow older, to slip away from the way we were brought up to be 'just' a good wife/mother and instead step out and do what we can to avoid the coming catastrophe. These 'wisdom years' are a good time to do it.

One path, as older women of wisdom, is simplification. Having less 'stuff' to look after gives us more time to get on with what needs doing.

And where does the energy we need for this come from? Primarily, from healthy eating, though energy is about more than food. Keeping active, both mentally and physically, is important. We need to remain involved in favourite activities and to try new ones. Above all: nurturing friends and enjoying their company.

This agenda may need a change in mindset, from unconscious negativity to something a little more cheerful. Even at the 11th hour, we can continue to develop our awareness of issues, viewpoints and unconscious biases, including our own.

KIM HOPE BECOMING A 'CRAFTIVIST'

If the Greenham Common Women's Peace Camp was still going strong, I'd go and live there semi-permanently rather than just the visits at weekends and during school holidays that I squeezed in between full-time teaching and looking after two children in the 1980s. As it is, I content myself with Extinction Rebellion and protesting outside the London Arms Fair. I haven't (yet?) joined Just Stop Oil, but I get their emails and each time I don't go on a protest I feel guilty. I'm not too keen on being sent to prison, but how else can I look my three grandchildren in the eye as the world continues to burn?

My excuse is not so much age (81) as the fact that I broke my back a while ago and so have less energy and more pain. Still, I would be able to go on protests if I 'girded my loins' – but I ask myself if it would really save the world or just make me feel better for having done something?

And then there's South Africa: I'll go back in January and see friends and some of the young people I worked with when I was running an HIV-prevention programme there more than a decade ago. It will be a poignant visit because I doubt I'll go again – I couldn't justify the air travel.

I will finalise my children's book: it's written, just needs lots of editing.

I'd like to see the Northern Lights and take a trip (by train) to Italy.

And I will revisit the creative/craft activities I once did – if I can turn my tiny spare room into an activities room/studio. I will become a 'craftivist'.

LIZ PUTTICK EMBRACING ACTIVISM

What do I still want to do? After a life in London, mostly working in publishing, I thought I had the answer: a move to the country, where I would live quietly and cultivate my garden, as Voltaire prescribed. At first I was happy, but soon I found I missed being part of the action. My life had meaning but lacked purpose.

I've always been a Labour voter but never found the time to get fully involved, apart from a few years as part of a workers' coop printers. I've always been a feminist too, but had expressed it mainly academically (PhD followed by writing and teaching on women and religion). But after my move to the country, I started to attend the meetings of our local Labour branch.

My involvement escalated under the latest boundary changes, when we moved from a solidly Tory constituency to a winnable battleground seat. I was drawn into campaigning through the excitement of the parliamentary-candidate selection process – though as an introvert, canvassing didn't come easily. It helped that people were polite even if they didn't like our politics, and sometimes we had friendly and productive conversations on the doorstep.

I had no intention of volunteering for a post, but at the AGM of our Constituency Labour Party (CLP) no one else put their hand up. I thought, 'I could do this!' and my hand rose almost involuntarily, with the result that I emerged from the meeting as the CLP women's officer. I've been in the role only a few months, but I'm already making plans to improve conditions for women within the constituency and to encourage more women to go for leadership roles.

The surprise July 2024 election was exhilarating if exhausting. We all worked really hard, and the joy of victory is indescribable. For the first time in history, Banbury has a Labour MP, Sean Woodcock, and the whole of Oxfordshire has shifted from Tory to either Labour or Lib Dem.

I feel there's a lot to be said for becoming politically active later in life. Not only do you bring a lifetime's experience, but you are better able to step back from the drama and stress, partly because it's voluntary work rather than career-building so there's less at stake personally, freeing you to focus on the bigger picture. Another unexpected bonus is the camaraderie of working with a committed, energetic and friendly team towards a common purpose and for a greater cause.

So I'm happy to have found the meaning and purpose I was looking for. I feel more engaged again with national and world events, however depressing and enraging. My only regret is not having embarked on this path earlier in my life, and I have huge admiration for younger women who somehow carve out time from their busy personal and professional lives for public service.

GERRIE TER HAAR REAL LIFE

The older I get the busier, or at least so it feels. Since my retirement many years ago, a natural process of unwinding has set in that has brought its own agenda with its own priorities. After a successful career as an academic, I feel a special responsibility to support a new generation of upcoming scholars, as well as to family, friends and others having to live not by choice but by circumstance. Hence the question for me is not just what I *want* to do, but what *needs* to be done, despite my personal preferences.

Real life is full of demands and responsibilities we cannot escape from, also not as we get older. The increasing need to support friends and family is rewarding yet also time-consuming, time that I would otherwise want to devote to quiet reading, for example – I think of the many books that are waiting to inspire me and feed my soul at a time when hopes of a better future seem beyond realisation. The need for political action seems greater than ever – not something I like to get involved in directly but which I cannot entirely refrain from. Human rights, in particular, has always been a topic close to my heart, both as an activist and as an academic.

On the publication of his recent book *Das Späte Leben* (lit. The Late Life), the German writer Bernhard Schlink, a former law professor and career judge, reflected on his life at almost 80 years old. He comes to the conclusion that life in old age is still *real* life: an intense life with its own challenges and problems, but also with its own joy.

I could not agree more.

RUTH HILTON
I JUST WANT TO CARRY ON

Sixty was a long time ago. Back then my husband had dropped dead, my child had left home, I had an active social/cultural life, was involved in charity work and continued to be employed as a PSHE Advisory Teacher by Brighton, Hove and East Sussex. I'd been forced to go part time after restructuring but had picked up another project for the Participation Team. I had no intention of anything changing just because I'd hit another round-number birthday.

A few years later I was dumped by the local authority and had to make decisions about my future. I knew I needed a sense of purpose, was arrogant enough to believe I still had something to offer and was in the process of preparing a consultancy flyer when my Mum had an accident and I had to take over running her business and managing her care. I was already committed to consultancy work in local schools but dealing with Mum's affairs meant being in London each week, which enabled me to accept offers of work and social activities there as well.

I was busy and active, generally felt fulfilled, and had no intention of anything changing. Then Mum died and along came lockdown. Now pushing 80, I am still chair of a charity, a school governor, actively involved in the Sex Education Forum and go to gigs and the theatre frequently. These projects and activities help me to feel valued and combat any feelings of isolation and loneliness. I just want to carry on with everything I'm involved with and hope my ageing body doesn't prevent that happening!

MARGIE MITCHELL
OLD BAG, NEW BAG

For the last decade, I have often declared myself to be a non-acquisitional person. 'I want fewer things not more...' I say smugly. I tell my friends that I never shop except for essentials. What a tiresome friend I must be!

On the way back from the Saatchi Gallery, I walk by the doors of Aria, one of the more expensive shops in Islington. There, in the display window, lies a solitary zip bag with straps designed to allow it to function either as a rucksack or a carry bag.

The gorgeous, solitary zip bag beckons me.

I ask the man serving to measure it to see if it complies with Wizz Air regulations. It doesn't: every measurement is five centimetres too big. I explore the radiant green, royal blue and grey external pockets, already, in my head, inserting keys, passport, credit cards, tissues, lip balm. I tuck my laptop into the internal pocket, throw in a bathing suit, a few pairs of knickers and before I know it, I'm sitting on a dusty road somewhere in the region of Tikal in Guatemala, where indigenous ladies troop past in national costume, occasionally nodding, but just as often oblivious to the not-particularly-young reddish-haired woman with a beautiful bag.

'He---llo...' says the measuring man, with a question mark on his big friendly face. He returns my bag to the platform in the display window.

I spend the next 12 hours wanting, aching with want: *jabberty, jibberty, stabberty stab*.

I sleep through the night, travelling old haunts

with my blue-pocketed bag. I chug down the Rio San Juan, swim deep in the cenotes of the Yucatan, drink horchatas with a liquid-eyed stranger. I fill my blue bag with gifts for the children in San Pedro hospital, *God bless you, sweet Rufina, take this dolly.* In Quetzaltenango, the street kids from the dormitorio take me to a remote market scattered across the base of the Santa Maria volcano; we buy a handful of swimming trunks and stuff them into the side pockets of my bag before setting off for the cloud forest and the hot springs of Fuentes Georginas.

The next day, I walk into Aria and buy the bigger-than-I-need bag. I will take it on Berrys Coach to Somerset next weekend, fill it with sensible shoes, a warm sweater and a few treats for my sister with dementia.

VICKY WILSON ZERO WASTE

When I was in my late 20s, the man I was married to died. He was 42. My grief was as much for him – for a life cut short – as for myself.

The only sane response seemed to be to recognise my own life as a gift and to use it as well as possible. The feeling resolved itself into a habit of asking myself, every so often, 'If I had only months to live, what from the last two years would I regret wasting time on?'

Now, at almost 70, when the likelihood of dying in two (or maybe even ten) years is greater, it suddenly seems more urgent to reach a state of zero waste of my life. With no need to build a future career, I accept work only when it is pleasurable or well paid (providing for more pleasure). An increase in anxiety, reduction in the desire to experience everything life can offer and awareness of the harm done by mass tourism means I've abandoned any ambitious travel plans. And I'm becoming more selfish. I'm learning to say no.

So what do I still want to do? I believe my legacy lies not in books I've written but in memories I've helped to create – so talk and laugh, eat and drink with people I care about. Enjoy my body – through dance, Pilates and walking. Dig, weed and deadhead. Explore (and sometimes write about) cities and landscapes, new and familiar. Be transfixed by live music and the big screen. Lose myself in pages of fictional lives. Help out where I can – and fight the political poisons spread across our world. Be a mother and grandmother, a friend, partner and lover.

ARIANA GEE GIRLS R US

My very dear friend got sick on the day of my 60th birthday. I called the ambulance and cancelled my party. Two weeks later I was with her in Mexico as she underwent a last desperate naturopathic attempt to kick the cancer she had been struggling with for years. It didn't work and three weeks later she died.

I was 70 in April. I didn't try for a party this time. I've been spending the whole year celebrating, starting with a seven-week trip to India. Several more friends have died. I'm still here and I'm grateful and excited about life. I don't take it for granted. Every new day feels like a bonus.

In my 60s, I sold my business, trained as a yoga therapist and decided to change my sexual orientation. I loved a woman for eight years, although sadly, our relationship ended almost a year ago. This year, aged 70, I went on the dating app Bumble and swiped right (being careful not to swipe left!) on some amazingly interesting women: a psychotherapist, a professor, an architect, a climate-change activist, a theatre director, a mindfulness teacher, to name but a few. After my marriage broke up way back when, and I did (now almost defunct) internet dating, the men I spoke to weren't half as interesting. Girls R Us is so much more fun than Boys R Us ever was.

Do I now need to identify myself as a lesbian? Why? I have been with men most of my life. And now I want to spend the rest of what is left with a woman. Labels might define for others who they think we are, but labels can also create separation. Surely a rose by any other name…?

HELEN AGUIRRE THE OFRENDA

I heard something on the radio the other day that made me think:

There is something magical when an experience enhances your life in such a way, that it becomes a comfort.

And I thought of the Ofrenda.

During my 13 years of living in Mexico, I experienced Ofrendas often: every year during the Day of the Dead celebrations, of course, but also more personally, as people I knew and loved died. The Ofrenda is a dedicated, individual, special place of recognition for us and for those who have gone. It is both a personal and a collective experience.

Many years ago, the father of my children died, aged 46. In true Mexican style, we set up an Ofrenda, for him and for us. His brother and family came over to the UK and we made the Ofrenda together, including their two very young children in the process, spending the day transforming a tall bookcase into a colourful life story.

At the centre is a smiling photograph. And from there, a spidergram of personal artefacts and objects, telling stories of a life, reaches upwards, downwards and sideways. There is a bowl of freshly made rice *a la mexicana* (his favourite). There is a cappuccino, a shot glass of Don Julio Añejo tequila and an ashtray of cigarette butts (our 15-year-old son's choice). A homemade corn tortilla sits next to a bowl of Hershey's Kisses chosen by our daughter. I place two treasured CDs on either side of the photograph, together with the hat and shoe from Monopoly. The other spaces are filled with objects that remind us of past times shared, and we laugh and dance and cry remembering.

Finally, the Ofrenda is framed with bright flowers and many candles. It is done and the letting go has begun.

The Ofrenda is a temporary event. My children each have a photograph of the original Ofrenda but mostly the anniversary of their father's death is marked by the wider Mexican/British family's WhatsApp messages.

In the years since, I have found solace in making other Ofrendas which have helped me to come to terms with the death of other loved ones. So I encourage anyone to celebrate a life well lived by making an Ofrenda: any place, any time, anyhow and with anyone.

As I grow older, it has become even more important that death is acknowledged in a thoughtful, participatory way. And it makes me glad to know that my children will have a source of comfort when their mother's death comes.

There really is something magical that happens, which then becomes a comfort.

SUE BLUNDELL THE MIXTURE AS BEFORE

So I went to see this fortune-teller my friend told me about. Took a pinch of salt like she'd said, a tin of salmon for her cat, a bottle of gin. And 50 quid, in tenners.

ME (*Sitting*) I'd like to know what to do with the rest of my life. I'm 77 now and time is running out.

FT Sorry, I only give yes or no answers.

ME That's a bit of a cop-out, isn't it?

FT No.

ME Please, can you tell me what I should focus on? Should I carry on writing…? Or go to live in Rome for six months…?

FT Yes.

ME Or should I spend more time with my friends…?

FT Yes.

ME Or Climate Action…? Yes, OK. Don't tell me. Climate Action too. (*Sighs*) You see, it's only in the last two years I've started to relax. It's the anti-anxiety pills, I wish I'd started them sooner. So maybe I should just enjoy myself? Read novels, potter about…?

FT No.

ME No! Why not? Well, I can see your point. Might be boring. (*Standing up*) Thank you, that was helpful. Quite like therapy, really. (*Rooting out another bottle of gin from her bag*) Why don't you have this as well…? (*Turning back at the door*) Do you think I will be remembered?

FT Yes.

ME Really?

FT For a while. Most people are.

KATHERINE UKLEJA
A LEGACY OF AWE AND SORROW

My grandmother was one of five sisters. Looking back to the 1920s, these women's lives were unusual: all of them sophisticated, educated to the hilt and highly successful in their chosen fields of endeavour – science, finance, diplomacy and the arts. My grandmother was the only homemaker among them. My mother was the only child.

I lean back into the vigour and inspiration of their combined brilliance. Yet I never met them, not one. It was only after my mother's death that their identity, shrouded in impenetrable secrecy over the decades, was disclosed. They were Jewish, a wealthy, erudite, secular family. They all perished in Poland, victims of Nazi barbarity.

The revelation stunned me and shattered my sense of identity. Twenty years on, I am still reeling. When I finally retire in 2026, 75 years young, I hope to spend my days making peace with my ancestry. To honour these significant women. To turn this unpardonable, crushing circumstance into a source of renewed creativity, a launchpad, not a stranglehold.

EM SAWDAY
A LINE OF STRONG WOMEN

In September last year I celebrated my 80th birthday. In December we downsized from the house we'd bought after we married, 48 years ago. Becoming 80 and that house-move flung me into gloom. We focused on age-proofing the new house, imagining carers living with us or perhaps with only one of us: visions of ourselves on the downward slope filled my view of the future. I was drowning, could feel my horizon closing in.

So when a friend mentioned in March that she was facilitating a psilocybin retreat in the Netherlands in a few weeks' time, I jumped.

My sons talked about the transformative world of the magic mushroom. Maybe I'd find I could be transformed too?

Come with a question you want to explore, something you hope for.

My question: How do I live this part of my life well?

My hope: To accept this age and stage of life.

Terror and intrigue build equally as the first day of taking the potion arrives. Terror takes over as I sip it. What-ifs crowd my mind. What if I addle my brain further? Never come back from the trip? What if my ego won't let go?

Once the potion takes hold of me, however, there is no discussion with ego. First my brain, then my entire body feels electrified, as if every nerve-ending is fired up. Visions of snakes like Medusa's curls wind themselves before me: their translucent bodies glow, their ruby and diamond eyes gaze at me and then they are gone in the twist of a tail.

All change. A grandmother I have never met steps forward. My mother stands in front of her, I stand below her, and below me is our baby daughter, who died two days after she was born. Dancing in front of us all is my nine-year-old granddaughter. The line of strong women in my family: I see that those who come before give life to those who follow. It is the order of things and I am part of this order.

I receive this message several times, in different forms, on the five-day retreat. I am transformed in ways I didn't imagine. I feel settled, no longer drowning, my horizon expanded.

There is still time for adventures.

MARCELLE DELVAUX-ABBOTT
FUN WHEN YOU TURN 60

I turned 60 last year and it felt quite liberating. So I decided to mark the year by doing 60 things I'd never done before. Here is the list of things I've managed so far:

1. Going to the top of the cathedral to look at the city where I live from a different angle.
2. Running through the municipal fountain.
3. Accepting a dinner invitation from someone I don't appreciate to please a member of my family.
4. Buying the first skirt of my life and accepting the shape of my body.
5. Spending the day in a spa with my friend instead of preparing for work.
6. Stopping biting my fingernails.
7. Colouring my nails bright orange.
8. Watching a movie on my own instead of working.
9. Doing ChatGPT / AI training for teachers.
10. Refusing to drink a glass of good wine in a plastic cup during a party. (Saying 'no' instead of 'yes, thank you'.)
11. Looking after an ageing and aggressive parent-in-law with empathy.
12. Charging an electric car.
13. Buying a Christmas decoration in September.
14. Ordering food online.
15. Going to the Chelsea Flower Show.
16. Reading an instruction leaflet all the way through.
17. Deciding to like dogs. It worked!
18. Doing an embroidery saying: 'I love dogs.'

19. Going to a Pride parade.
20. Refusing some work.
21. Saying 'no' to members of my family.
22. Organising our daughter's wedding.
23. Living in four countries in a year (for work).
24. Going to a nudist beach.
25. Having a singing lesson.
26. Driving a convertible car.
27. Wearing glitter on my face.
28. Going to Chicago for a week.
29. Learning five new English words per week (I am a French speaker).
30. Reading part of the Bible.
31. Saying thank you to people daily.
32. Slowing down when I feel tired.
33. Travelling only by public transport for six months.
34. Reading at least 60 paper pages per week.
35. Using only positive words.
36. Listening to people carefully without interfering.
37. Stopping worrying about my weight.
38. Having a meal with someone I met in a restaurant while he was waiting for a table.
39. Deciding to prioritise visiting friends abroad.
40. Having my writing published (thanks to Ida2).

So what do I still want to do? Learn Italian and basic Albanian; become familiar with sign language; run a training course on online resources for languages teachers; have a simulator flight experience; drive a canal boat; learn front crawl; read part of the Koran; take dance classes.

And as almost all the first 40 things were spontaneous, I'm leaving some possibilities open.

SALLY SPINKS CHANGES

Turning 60 marked a positive milestone. Giving up full-time work and moving house have changed my life beyond compare. And, of course, HRT patches have made a contribution to that feeling of a weight being lifted.

I had travelled extensively for my job and was constantly stressed and busy. There was never time to enjoy home or relaxation because there were always boring house and admin things to do. Since the changes in my life, I've discovered a love of pottering in the garden and I've even made jam. I question whether I've become the thing I never wanted to be: a middle-class homemaker. But I've also had more time for my husband, family and friends. And most excitingly, I've been able to pursue my passion and purpose through art.

But I do wonder how I can give back without getting sucked into a work-like commitment? There is so much wrong with the world – but where to start?

Increasingly, I'm also interested in what work culture in the UK does to people – especially women. Having the luxury of only working a few days here and there has given me perspective on the life I used to lead. I was defined by my job. I was driven to achieve as much as I could and as a result possibly burnt out at a time in my life when the menopause was raging. What was making me throw myself into work like this? Was it my own desire to succeed and please or was it societal expectation?

And most importantly, what can we do to bring about a discussion that leads to change?

LINDSAY MACRAE NOW WE ARE 63

I've stopped putting half the stuff I've done on my CV. It gives my age away. Do employers want to know that I worked on a pig farm, was a newsreader for the Vatican and took away bottles of pee from Shane MacGowan's bedroom in my role as his publicity manager? Are these transferable skills? I think so. I think no experience is wasted, which is why my tendency to say 'Yes!' to every job opportunity made for an interesting life but no pension. I need to work, but job offers seem to evaporate when you pass 60.

This is how I ended up (at the age of 62) as a Health Care Assistant on a busy cardiac ward. After being made redundant in 2022, I applied for countless jobs. All was well until the interview, when enquiries about my 'stamina' and 'energy' revealed the indirect ageism our society is riddled with.

The NHS had no such qualms – a woman who could remember Morecambe and Wise, isn't bothered by being called 'pet' and who has been through several bereavements and health emergencies was seen as an asset. They were also desperate.

My low-ranking job grants me the privilege of being with fellow humans during the worst moments of their lives. I feel energised, relevant and useful. My colleagues are diverse and skilled and there's no time for bitching and bullshit. The 13-hour shifts are exhausting (but the 25-year-olds are exhausted too) plus I'm getting in 25,000 steps a day so I'm saving on gym membership. Do I want to go on wiping arses and tears and being invisible to doctors who are younger than my children? Strangely, yes.

GRISHMA SUTARIA RETIREMENT

I always intended to retire as the headteacher of a primary school at the age of 55, to pursue my hobbies from days gone by. This finally happened on 31 December 2019, at the age of 56. After almost 14 years of working all hours, six or seven days a week, I realised it was time to let someone younger, with more energy, step into the role. (Cracks were appearing at home too, and I was beginning to struggle to cope with both.) My sister, a midwife manager, warned me not to give up a full-on job and go straight to nothing. But that's exactly what I did.

I lasted six weeks, hating the fact that my life now had no purpose. I was so used to making a difference to young people's lives, to getting through OFSTED inspections successfully, to acting as a seconded headteacher to support struggling schools – to name but a few of my many 'hats'. Now I felt as if I no longer had anything to look forward to.

So I decided to go back to work as a teacher for three and a half days a week, doing the job I first came into the profession to do and pursuing my main passion, which is to teach. I have since worked as an acting headteacher and seconded executive leader, but now, at 61, I am just a part-time supply teacher, based at a school that it gives me great pleasure to be part of.

I will eventually retire, but have given myself time to find out exactly how and what I want as a purpose in my life, in which I can make some small difference to myself and others around me.

MARIE MULVEY-ROBERTS
IS THERE LIFE AFTER RETIREMENT?

Soon, I will be leaving my full-time lecturing job. It was not until redundancies were announced that the idea of retiring really occurred to me as I realised that I needed to take voluntary severance to protect the jobs of younger colleagues. As one retiree put it, it is not until you finally leave the workplace that you become aware of all the stresses you have been carrying. I am looking forward to being free from a timetable, having no more marking, and relishing the space to write my long-delayed biography on women's suffrage.

So what else will retirement bring? I intend to continue being involved with projects around menopause so I can keep reminding menopausal women of how things can only get better. Sharing that world with them, beyond the hot flushes, brain fog, sleepless nights and roller-coaster of hormones, feels oddly rejuvenating. I even feel more connected to my pre-pubescent girlhood, which is a blessing.

I am lucky to be in good health, despite having spent so much of my life chained to a computer, though my current lack of exercise has to change. I am most excited about getting back into playing the pipe organ for long spells: right now, I only have time to learn a few hymns to play in a local church.

Apart from losing my interest in adrenaline sports, it seems that there is not much that age prevents me from doing.

HELEN LINDSAY-BREAKSPEAR
TIME AND WORDS: EMERITA

They say that most people dream about where they expect to be in five years' time. I wonder why we dream of the future rather than living in the present?

Burnt out from a profession I loved, working in secondary education, I began to imagine a time that consisted of early retirement, a garden, a cottage, a simple life. Five years on, and I'm living that dream. Yet I still feel the need for a 'third age', feel I've more to give.

I'm conscious of time now in a way I wasn't in my 40s and 50s. I still have my ambitious streak: I still want to 'create' and achieve, to design gardens, to write, study, paint, read, walk. I have things to do!

In interviews for new staff, we would ask where candidates saw themselves in five years' time. Why is it always five years? Yet I too find myself looking forward five years to when I'll get my state pension. I'm doing it again – failing to live in the moment.

It's a dilemma I've created for myself – a dilemma of time and words. At work, I always had a title, so is the lack of a title now the issue? I don't like the word 'retired', with its connotations of being put out to pasture, like a race horse. Perhaps I am a Senior Assistant Principal Emerita?

I need to *find* words for it, to define myself and dream of today.

I have a kernel of an idea. I'm going to forge ahead with it, right now!

FIONA DUBY WHO KNOWS?

The 60-year benchmark passed by me 14 years ago. I hadn't even considered that I would stop working as a freelance consultant in international development: the job offers were constant and ever more interesting. I found the visuals of age were a bonus too, creating the illusion of credibility and trust, and at 60, eyes, ears and limbs were in good working order.

The combination of ending a job I didn't enjoy, the Covid lockdown and the care of a mother of nearly 103 confirmed that at nearly 70, I was ready to embark on my new life of 'retirement'. Daily yoga, a healthy diet, good physical and mental health and the prospect of a new relationship allowed me to believe that the following decade would be action-packed, with my bucket list being ticked off rapidly.

Mother died, lockdown ended, the new partnership was forged. Then arthritic aches and pains hit hard, hearing diminished and dental implants were proposed. Even gentle yoga was challenging. Keys, specs, phone and memory were frequently elusive. It all seemed to happen so quickly. Perhaps continuing to work had kept these all at bay?

Now at 74, the bucket list is still as lengthy, the relationship travels along an occasionally rocky road smoothed by compromise and communication, the hip is titanium and the swollen fingers ringless. But life is good, and I am ever grateful for all I have.

Turning 60, you may have ten precious years of maturity and expertise combined with physical fitness. Turning 70 is a different matter – and the following decade, well, who knows?

EILEEN CAMPBELL
LIVING CREATIVELY

As I slowly come to consciousness and let go of the night's dreams, I remind myself how fortunate I am. Still here, and healthy, when so many relatives and friends no longer are. Granted, the whole process of getting up in the morning takes longer than it used to, but routine helps – yoga, followed by coffee and a light breakfast. Each new day is a gift, and an opportunity to live creatively and meaningfully.

I review the tasks that need to be done, and most importantly what I would like to do for myself today. If the tasks are the weft of my life, then my interests and hobbies (literature, writing, music, art, gardening, cooking, other cultures and travel) are the warp. I'm driven by curiosity and passion, and my aim is to live as full a life as possible.

Since I'm not good at coping with disorder, I like to ensure that everything in the house and garden is as 'pukka' as I can get it. The tasks sometimes seem endless, and finding that balance between doing what I deem necessary and doing what truly nourishes my wellbeing is a challenge.

I believe that each of us is responsible for the quality of our lives and for finding meaning and purpose in how we spend our time. So focusing on what's important to me and managing my energy to make sure I don't exhaust myself with needless distraction or procrastination is vital. Making space for the creative pursuits that nurture me means making choices and prioritising my activities. We all need to ensure that we feed our souls!

It seems that if we want to live a rich and creative life, we need to respect process rather than become obsessed with achievement. This applies to mundane tasks too. So if I can elevate my ordinary, everyday duties into something meaningful through awareness, rather than see them as irritating necessities that get in the way of my creativity, then I feel more at ease. That means I try to extract the same enjoyment as I get from creative pursuits by mindfully washing the dishes, cleaning, weeding or whatever I need to do. I try to flow – to work through a task, digest the experience and move on.

As we begin to wind down towards old age, this phase of our life can teach us what we need to learn – to slow down, to pay attention, to surrender to the flow of life and to accept that we cannot control everything. Rather, perhaps we can make the most of our time and live creatively, living in the here and now, whatever we are engaged in.

VICCI JOHNSON HAPPY BEING ME

I have awakened to the joy of being me – I am no longer thinking 'what should I do with the next phase of my life?' or 'am I doing enough for other people?' I've realised that re-purposing my life now that I'm 61 doesn't require me to seek out what to do next – it will just happen and feel right at the time. My true wealth lies in the joy of being. And if I can share this joy, then my legacy will be in other people's happiness.

I get joy from keeping my body fit and healthy while exercise gives my life structure and interest. And helps me to feel alive.

I want to connect more to the natural world, feel the earth beneath my feet, seek out aspects of nature that lift my heart – bird migration, shooting stars, the Northern Lights, full moons, spring tides and birdsong. And share this love with my grandchildren, as my mother did with my own children. I want to show my compassion for our planet and do what I can to protect its fragile existence.

I value hugely spending time with family and friends – making memories to be cherished forever.

I feel incredibly lucky that I have freedom, time, a lovely home, enough money and am surrounded by love, so I can follow my dreams. I am looking forward to more spontaneity, silliness and adventure.

And when people ask me how old I am, I might just say 'old enough to be a grandmother but young enough to run naked into the sea'.

MARY ALLEN
SIMPLICITY, PATIENCE, COMPASSION

I'm 73 years young and have had a life packed with adventure. I've been both an actor and director, have worked for a multinational oil company and have travelled the world. I was the CEO of two major arts organisations, married to two City boys who became artists, couldn't have children but have two fabulous step-children. Most importantly, I now write poetry. I have won an award, and I'm doing an MA at the Poetry School. The key to my life now is in this excerpt from one of my poems about masks:

…the most powerful and effective mask is old age.
    Some women complain of invisibility.
For me it is the source of my power: I am become
    ordinary, unimportant, non-existent,
evaporated. I am beyond others' actions, I can watch
    the world, do exactly
what I want. I have become wholly irrelevant, finally
    my own Self.

What do I want to do now? Stop still and meditate. Strengthen and build up my poetry. Find a remote cottage and spend two months there in silence. I want to deepen my friendships – have fewer friends with whom I have stronger relationships – yet be open to meeting new people with whom I resonate strongly. I have stage 4 metastatic cancer, but my oncologist tells me I still have years to live. The *Tao Te Ching* tells us that the most important qualities are simplicity, patience and compassion. I want to follow those, sometimes surrounded by friends, and sometimes in solitude.

DEBBIE THORPE
A MORE CENTRED LIFE

In a month's time I'll be 70. But the big change in my life has nothing to do with age: a late diagnosis of Lyme disease in my early 60s has wreaked havoc with my body's energy.

The most profound part of this process was reaching a point of acceptance of the situation I found myself in. That meant letting go of the pioneering, ambitious person who had a never-ending supply of ideas to create a 'successful' life.

The process has been both painful and liberating. The liberation lies in being able to focus on what feels important without needing to achieve specific goals. It seemed like an early life-lesson for later years.

During lockdown, Chris Packham and Megan McCubbin's daily broadcasts, *The Self-Isolating Bird Club*, deepened my commitment to wildlife and my awareness of the impact of both relentless economic growth and climate change.

As I enter my 70s, of course there are places I'd like to go (but no more long-haul flights) and my interests remain many and varied. But I want to live not at the many attractive edges, but more centred in what really matters to me, aligned with the meditation method I practise.

A recent decision to move to Edinburgh is as much a yearning for the wildlife Scotland offers as finding a place where culture, friends and amenities are a short walk or bus ride away.

It's the journey not the destination.

MIDORI NISHIKAWA BIONIC WOMAN

I have now recovered from Long Covid, after some medical intervention, various alternative therapies and a great deal of sleeping.

After a new left hip and a full hysterectomy in 2023, I now consider myself a new Bionic Woman.

At 72, I try to remind myself each morning as I get up that this is 'another holiday morning', which seems to take the immediacy out of what I consider to be 'chores'.

I believe I have never been a lazy person, therefore this amazes my husband, who has had to adapt to the NEW more laid-back me.

I do not beat myself up any more for not creating / painting 'this day'. I know I am an artist; I live my life as one.

I have re-learnt to look after my older body, marvelling at how it still works so hard for me.

I have learnt to work out more gently, to oil my joints. I try hard to make special time for myself (I still find this hard).

I hope that lots of people who have been lucky enough to come out of a long illness of any sort experience what I am still living with.

Feeling slightly euphoric all of the time.

Long may it last!

WANDA WHITELEY
THE GATE IN THE WALL

I've just turned 60, and with it came various losses and gains. This magic number has brought me a wonderful Wonka ticket in the shape of a 60+ Oyster card, but I've sustained several losses too, one after the other. My parents died recently, and my daughter leaves for university soon. I have gained my father's blind dog with bad breath and chattering teeth, who has somewhat clipped my wings, but perhaps that's a good thing: if I were any more unfettered, I'd float away.

No longer tethered by aged parents or a teenager, or joined at the hip to a partner, I find myself wishing for an uncluttered white bright space of my own, more Airbnb than family home. But floating away scares me. I come from a family with sturdy Northern origins, whose members pride themselves on taking dutiful community action. I could throw myself into something useful, too, but I'm cautious. Do I want to create new ties, new responsibilities? But without them, would I be a hedonist, drifting and purposeless?

So what next? My friend, who is 77, has the enviable position of living next to her daughter and grandchildren with – wait for it – a gate in the garden wall. This gate in the wall obsesses me. It sounds like something out of *The Secret Garden*; I imagine her grandchildren tumbling through it wearing Edwardian smocks. My daughter, aged 18, was horrified when I held out the tempting idea of forming our own hole-in-the-wall gang. 'You can forget that,' she said. 'I've already told you – I'm off to New York.'

I was very taken with legendary editor Diana Athill's decision, in her early 90s, to move into an old folk's home, full of genteel ladies who like books. But where are these places? I have also been looking into cooperative living ventures. Having taunted myself with the question of who will be my load-bearing person when I slide into decrepitude, I have come to the conclusion there might be safety in numbers. What if I were to hitch my wagon to a group of can-do women? Many of my friends profess to want to live in flatlets under one roof, a communal space where we would support each other (and laugh a lot). But would this really work? Or is it just a fantasy?

NANCY CHARLEY WHAT A GIFT!

Ida, thank you. Your theme has helped me to clarify some vague plans. I would like:

1. *To live in a place where the scenery awes.* I've no roots in any particular area so I would like my next move to be to a place that feeds me and my creativity.

2. *To archive some papers in a subject that fascinates.* I qualified as an archivist after raising my children and for the last ten years I've worked for the Royal Asiatic Society. Asian history holds no particular appeal for me, however, so before I hang up my archivist boots, I'd like to work on papers for a community or person that enchants me.

3. *To continue writing poetry and prose* that helps me, and hopefully others, to work though the joy and pain of living in this world.

4. *To explore my spirituality.* As an adolescent, I fell in love with a Father who loved me unconditionally. Since then my spiritual awareness has grown, shifted, been moulded and broken. In these later years I wish to understand more of spirituality, particularly in the areas of mysticism, lost female god(s) and how earth responds to our continuing desecration.

5. *To continue to craft.* It gives me great delight to dye, weave, knit, sew, make and create. I'd like to craft more, allowing myself time to play.

Play – that's the key. May whatever time I have left be filled with an attitude of play, finding joy in simple things, living lightly, caring for family and our wounded planet.

P.S. There are a couple more wants – but those will stay my secrets!

JOY FISHER
REVERSE BUCKET LIST

My dance partner Braude and I step carefully out of her car onto the pavement. It's Sunday afternoon; we should be in our dance class, but we have had to stop dancing. Instead, we've come for a slow stroll at the seaside.

Braude has been diagnosed with a torn meniscus in her right knee. Her doctor told her to avoid sudden twists and turns. Say goodbye to the tango! Truth be told, my own left knee has been hurting, too. According to a radio programme I heard recently, some time between age 70 and 75 most of us begin to lose muscle mass at an accelerated rate. Maybe we're just getting old.

We walk slowly along the esplanade, stopping from time to time at the memorial benches placed so old people like us can rest. I think about how many years I've loved dancing. I picture our dance teacher Elizabeth standing alone, her weight perfectly balanced over her own two feet; her admonition: 'NEVER lean on your partner!' What if I can never stand alone like that again? Will my dancing days be over? I feel bereft; something precious is being taken from me.

Braude will have none of it. She leads when we dance, and she leads now. 'We will dance again,' she insists. 'In the meantime, let's make a reverse bucket list.'

'A what?'

'You've heard of a bucket list? All the things you want to do before you kick the bucket?' I nod.

'Well, let's make a list of all the things we have an excuse not to do any more because of our knees.'

'Like what?'

She gazes out to sea, spots a sailboat. 'Like sailing,' she says. 'I never much liked sailing. All that rolling and heaving. Now I'll never have to go sailing again. Too hard on my knee, don't ya know.' She looks challengingly at me. 'What will you toss into your bucket?'

I'm silent, considering. Suddenly I remember an afternoon almost two decades earlier, a beautiful sunny Southern California day. I'd come down to Venice Beach, where roller-skaters glided in lazy curves along serpentine sidewalks. Shifting their weight from side to side, they negotiated the path almost as if they were dancing. I hadn't been on roller skates since high school, but, on impulse, I approached the stall where they were for rent.

I laced the skates on, stood up – and started to roll! I couldn't remember how to stop properly, so I fell down instead, scraping my knee on the rough concrete. Inches from my eyes, grains of silica in the sidewalk twinkled in the sunlight, as if laughing at the middle-aged fool sprawled above them.

'I never have to go roller-skating again,' I crow to Braude, with a certain sense of satisfaction.

Together, we contemplate the many possibilities for saying 'no' inherent in the surprisingly liberating concept of the reverse bucket list. Having a reason to say no to things we don't want to do is a fine thing. But I am still troubled. I don't want to say no to dancing.

We are sitting on what I've come to think of as the 'dancer's bench'. The memorial plaque says the bench is dedicated to 'a courageous mother who chose to dance through the good and difficult times'. I suddenly realise that the reverse bucket list isn't just convenient for dumping unwanted activities. It's also good for rejecting inappropriate advice. If Braude and I can no longer maintain the perfect 'stand alone' posture Elizabeth demands of her dancers, that doesn't mean we should quit dancing. 'Courageous mother' didn't give up dancing during the difficult times, so why should Braude and I? Braude was right. We will dance again, if not perfectly, then as well as we can.

We rise from the bench and begin picking our way carefully back to the car, two ageing women, arm-in-arm, leaning – just a little – on each other.

ANN TRENEMAN OUT!

It began as a sudden urge as I sat in my front room, eyeing the floor-to-ceiling bookcase. 'Out!' I thought. These books – novels and poetry, history and gardens, photography and biography – had so long been my familiars. I had loved them not only for what they were but for the way they provided a map of my life – discovering journalism through Watergate, the words of Bob Dylan, well-worn maps of the Peak District. Now I saw them in a different light. They felt heavy, freighted with memory and, in that way that some autobiographies can be, self-regarding.

So 'Out!' it was. At least 300 went to charity but I wanted to keep about 100 – just not in the front room (the bookcase sold almost instantly on Facebook). Then I remembered, as if I hadn't already known, that there was another bookcase, in another room, that at some heady point had been re-designated as the 'drinks cupboard'. I opened its glass doors and looked, in something close to awe, at the collection of glasses and booze. Those were the party days. Sherry and wine glasses, flutes and snifters. Voluptuous shapes for margaritas, elegant stiletto stems for cocktails. All but ten went to charity. Many of the bottles were decades old: triple sec, ouzo, brandy, crème de cassis, Martini, Pernod, Malibu, sherry, tequila, etc. Most went down the drain – glug glug – with no regrets. The books fit perfectly.

This small story is what I thought of when I asked the question: 'What do I still want to do?' I want a life less encumbered by the past. The word that resonates is 'simplify'. It's not very dramatic, but it's powerful.

Thank you again to everyone who has engaged with The Ida Project.

If you would like to order copies of this book, or join in with the conversation, please get in touch.
By email: info@theidaproject.com
By post: 73 Tower Road South,
Bristol BS30 8BW

You can also order copies of our first book, *Is This What We Expected?*, with contributions by 30 women about life after 60, from the same email or address for £5 (plus p&p).

First published in 2024 for
The Ida Project
info@theidaproject.com
by Categorical Books, 73 Tower Road South,
Bristol BS30 8BW

Copyright © 2024 the contributors
ISBN 978-1-904662-27-3
A CIP record for this book is available from the British Library

Printed in the UK by Dayfold Group